Marcos Paulo Riccioni de Melos

Vehicle Traffic Simulation on Graphics Cards with CUDA

Marcos Paulo Riccioni de Melos

Vehicle Traffic Simulation on Graphics Cards with CUDA

Application based on the Cellular Automata Model

ScienciaScripts

Imprint

Any brand names and product names mentioned in this book are subject to trademark, brand or patent protection and are trademarks or registered trademarks of their respective holders. The use of brand names, product names, common names, trade names, product descriptions etc. even without a particular marking in this work is in no way to be construed to mean that such names may be regarded as unrestricted in respect of trademark and brand protection legislation and could thus be used by anyone.

Cover image: www.ingimage.com

This book is a translation from the original published under ISBN 978-613-9-68767-1.

Publisher:
Sciencia Scripts
is a trademark of
Dodo Books Indian Ocean Ltd. and OmniScriptum S.R.L publishing group

120 High Road, East Finchley, London, N2 9ED, United Kingdom
Str. Armeneasca 28/1, office 1, Chisinau MD-2012, Republic of Moldova, Europe
Printed at: see last page
ISBN: 978-620-8-22961-0

Summary

Thanks

To all those who have helped me in some way to complete this important phase of my life, which will be the first step towards my first million.

SUMMARY

Vehicle Traffic Simulation on Graphical Plazas
Marcos Paulo Riccioni de Melos

December/2014

Advisor: Juliana Mendes Nascente e Silva, D.Sc. DCC - IM - UFRRJ

Cellular automata (CA) is a technique used in complex and dynamic systems, where the solution of problems is discretized, governed by simple and deterministic rules, with expressive results. CAs can be used to describe biological systems, as in the case of the Game of Life (Gol), simulating the self-reproduction of organisms. Another use of CAs is for forecasting and planning vehicular traffic (TAC) on highways and in urban centers. However, these simulations demand a lot of processing time, requiring high computing power. In this context, GPUs (Graphics Processing Units) enable massively parallel processing, so that the SIMD (Sigle Instruction Multiple Data) architecture provided by GPUs is suited to the implementation structure of CAs. This results in a parallelization mode that enables a significant improvement in the model's performance. This work aims to study CAs, proposing parallelization methodologies for two applications of the technique, following the specifications described above. The results showed that the improvement in the Goal was significant, indicating the possibility that it could also be used in the TAC at a later date. Therefore, this work has provided a better understanding of the behavior of parallelization on graphics cards with CUDA, using the CA technique.

Chapter 1

Introduction

A simulation is a mathematical model capable of representing reality in a simplified way and can be used to predict and/or interpret certain scenarios. These simulations are based on rules that govern the nature of the problem and can be used in a wide variety of areas of knowledge.

Among the simulation techniques is the Cellular Automaton (CA), which is used in complex dynamic systems, where the system is discretized and described using simple rules. It is a technique that brings out the global behavior of the simulated system from local interactions. CAs have been used in simulators since the 1990s, as it is a simple technique that produces significant results. [18]

The CA technique is generic and can be used for a wide range of simulations in the most diverse areas of knowledge, such as forest fire modeling, or physical models such as Ising's, cryptography, disease dispersion, among many other problems. [10, 17]

CA was proposed by John Von Neumann with the aim of modeling a self-reproducing system, where the idea was for a robot to be able to build another copy of itself from a set of separate parts. In 1983, CA gained ground with the work of Stephen Wolfram, who proposed complex systems obtained through elementary rules. John Von Neumann, with the help of Stanislaw Ulam, proposed a cellular automaton model capable of simulating self-reproduction. [10,21]

In the mid-1970s, John Horton Conway proposed a pioneering work using CA to describe a biological system. This work became known as the Game of Life (Gol), which simulates the self-reproduction of biological organisms. Other complex dynamic systems have also been modeled using CAs, one of which is vehicular traffic (TAC). In this case, the characteristics of traffic are very well reproduced through a set of elementary rules, which allows a good understanding of the dynamics of vehicle flow, making it possible to simulate both traffic on highways and in urban centers. [13,15, 18, 24]

CA generates a dynamic or complex system based on local interactions, which requires greater computational power when forecasting systems are simulated. In this way, the characteristics of each scenario can also affect computing time, such as the vehicle simulation of the city of Rio de Janeiro, where the size of the system directly affects computing time.

Simulation systems can be predictive, where given a current state of the system, you can know how the system will evolve over a short period of time. Another application of simulation is in relation to the correct understanding of the simulated system. In the first case, a forecasting system, computing power is essential and, in this sense, to forecast vehicle traffic, parallel and distributed computing is necessary, because if the response time is longer than the real time, the simulation will give outdated information about the system being studied. Based on this demand, parallel programming is proposed to improve the application's performance.

A very current aspect of parallel programming is the use of graphics cards (GPU - Graphics Processor Unit) for general processing, due to their processing capacity and low cost. Initially, Graphics Processor Units (GPU) were developed to carry out tasks related to problems in the field of Computer Graphics, such as transformations on a mesh of vertices or shades of a pixel, processing these tasks in milliseconds and faster than the CPU. This hardware is highly specialized in massively parallel processing, as it has a large number of processing units or cores capable of executing the same instruction on different data. [8,14,20]

Because CAs are explicit in time, this application is very suggestive of the parallelism available in GPUs. With this, in a single time step, it is possible to compute the change in state of all the cells (vehicles) at the same time, made possible by the non-dependence of data at each time step.

This paper proposes a parallelization methodology for implementing a CA that simulates the Gol. A study of the TAC is also carried out, so that all the variables can be scrutinized, leading to a greater understanding of the problem, with the aim of improving its performance, with a process similar to that carried out on the Gol. [13, 18, 24]

1.1 Motivation

Cellular Automata is a simple and generic technique, which results in data with a high rate of accuracy, so knowledge of the technique makes it possible to understand and study various problems.

The Game of Life uses CAs to model a problem that is considered easy to understand and code, and was chosen to validate the improvement in its performance with the use of GPUs. In addition to this, a model that simulates real needs is also studied, the TAC simulates a need that is increasingly present in large cities, which is the study of traffic, for possible adaptations of roads to new traffic conditions, which are increasingly saturated.

The models represent the logical part of the problem, but the input data of these systems can be large, resulting in the need for a great deal of computing power, requiring time to learn the result, solutions in the implementation are also necessary, based on the structures of the problems and the modeling technique. GPU programming is added as a tool for the faster solution of simulations carried out by CAs.

1.2 Objectives

After studying the problems, modeling techniques and parallelization techniques, one of the objectives of this work was to evaluate different cellular automata implementations that involve parallel programming on graphics cards, in order to improve performance. Another objective was to use a simple model to assess whether there is an improvement in performance with the use of GPUs and then apply the results to a real model.

Chapter 2

Cellular Automata

The cellular automata approach, also known as the finite state machine, was proposed by the German mathematician Stanislaw Ulam and the Hungarian mathematician John Von Neuman in the early 1950s. At the time, John Von Neuman was developing a system capable of self-replication and capable of reproducing self-producing mechanisms. Ulam observed that this mechanism created complex and sometimes self-similar structures. Using these principles, Von Neumann found that the simple CA mechanism was capable of generating highly complex structures. [3, 5, 6, 9, 10, 21, 22]

A CA consists of an infinite (computationally finite) regular grid of cells, each of which can be in a finite number of states, which vary according to deterministic rules. The change of state of each cell is made according to its current state, the state of the neighboring cells and through the transition function. Thus, the CA can be defined by a set (L, N, S and f), where:

- L, represents the discretization on a regular grid, formed by cells (c) of spatial dimension D;

- S is the finite set of states that the cell can assume;

- N is the adopted neighborhood such that $c \in L \Rightarrow N(c) \in L$, e,

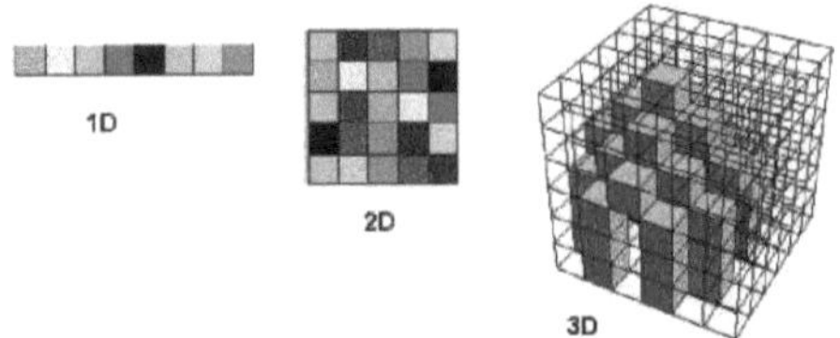

Figure 2.1: AC in 1, 2 and 3 dimensions. [10]

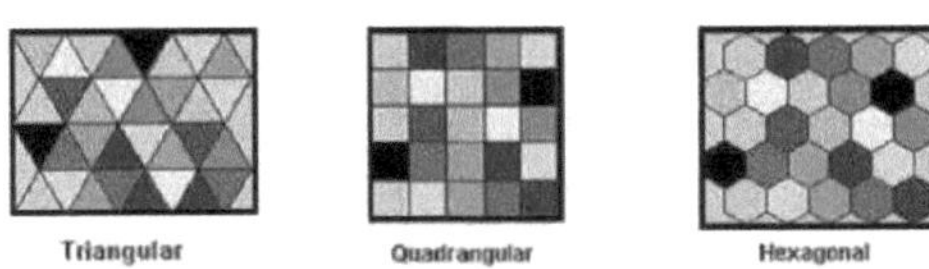

Figura 2.2:   Topologies: quadrangular, triangular and hexagonal. [10]

- f : (S,N) → S is the transition function.

ACs can be discretized in different topologies and in three dimensions as shown in Figures 2.1 and 2.2, these topologies and dimensions can be adapted to better represent each problem. [24]

This technique adapts very well to problems that discretize populations and simulate their extracellular interaction, i.e. each cell also needs information from the cells in its immediate vicinity to be able to perform the state change calculations, creating neighborhood links. These are updated every time the population interacts, after all the cells know their new state.

Time is also discretized, where the state of a cell at time t is obtained as a function of the state at time t - 1, taking into account its state and the states of neighboring cells.

This neighborhood corresponds to nearby cells that obey a predefined formation. Generally, problems are discretized computationally in the form of matrices, in which each element is one or more positions of the matrix. The most commonly used neighborhoods in 2D AC models are defined by Moore and Neumam,

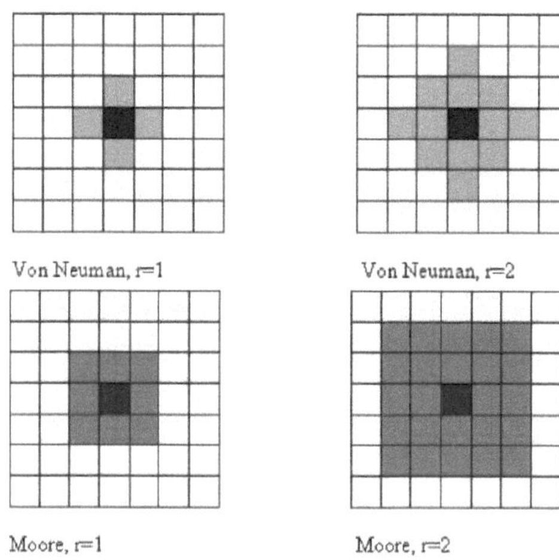

Figura 2.3:   Neighborhood according to Von Neuman and Moore. [10]

Figure 2.3 illustrates this neighborhood discretization with radius 1 and 2 [10,21].

Therefore, given a cell c and a radius r, the set of neighbors is defined as:

$$N(c) = r \in L; (c + r) \in L \tag{2.1}$$

From this discretization of the population, all the cells evolve following the same rules at each time step. Cell states are only updated after all cells have calculated their next state.

2.1 Game of life

Based on the models proposed by John Horton Conway, the theoretical application Gol (Game of Life) is presented. It reproduces, using simple rules, the alterations and changes in groups of living beings, illustrating the behavior of cells in relation to time and their environment. [9, 21]

Gol has only four rules:

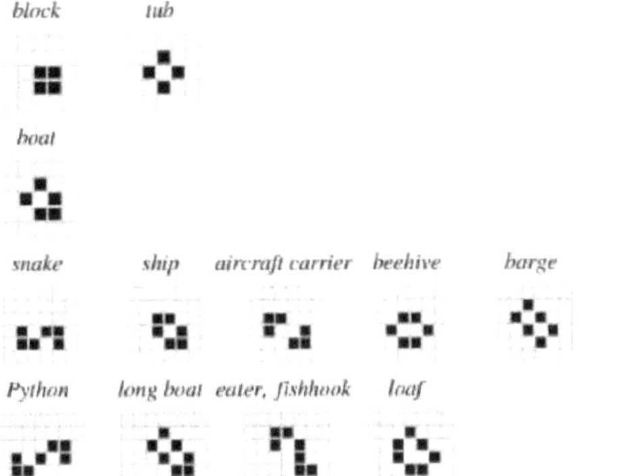

Figura 2.4:   Structures created by the Goal.

- Any living cell with fewer than two living neighbors dies of loneliness;

- Any living cell with more than three living neighbors dies of overpopulation.

- Any dead cell with exactly three living neighbors becomes a living cell.

- Any living cell with two or three living neighbors remains in the same state for the next generation.

According to the rules of the model, various structures are created, some of which can be seen in Figure 2.4. Each structure has a different shape and behavior, and can change according to its environment. [10]

The Goal can also be represented in three dimensions, which is a model closer to reality as it deals with all directions tangent to the cell being studied. All models have variables that are disregarded because they are not important to the focus of the work, or even in cases where the behavior of the variable is not known. In this case, the discretization into just 26 neighbors for each cell is a way of simplifying the model, given the need for a lot of computing power to calculate each cell. The three-dimensional representation

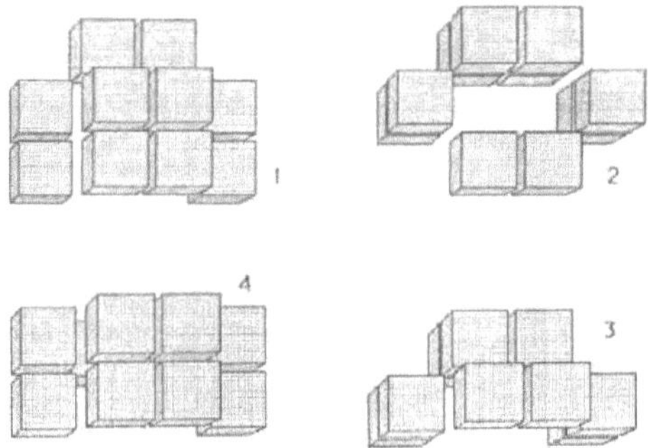

Figure 2.5: Goal in 3 dimensions.

can be seen in Figure 2.5, where the cells evolve over three generations after initialization. [1]

Other models have a similar structure to Gol, where each cell corresponds to just one individual in the entire simulation. For example, in the forest fire dispersal model, a cell corresponds to just one tree. In the TAC model, the cells are fractions of a track, not holding all the information for changing state, where it is just a structure for joining data from the other entities. Gol is a model with a different objective from TAC. However, the two models share the same programming logic, in which, by using parallel programming, the time elapsed from initialization to result should be reduced.

2.2 Cellular Automata Applied to Vehicle Traffic

The behavior of vehicular traffic has been studied extensively in recent decades by various fields of knowledge, such as engineering, mathematics, physics and others. In order to model vehicular traffic, it is necessary to have an understanding of the basic theory surrounding the modeling technique to be used. [23]

The modeling of vehicular traffic by CA has had many expressive results, due to its robustness, versatility and simplicity, managing to represent the dynamics of vehicular traffic as free flow or congested. This technique has been gaining the attention of researchers, especially since the 1990s, to model traffic on both highways and urban roads. [13, 18]

In CA traffic modeling, the position of each vehicle *i is* given by x_i and its speed by v_i. These variables, as well as the time variable t, are discrete in the model. The speed of each vehicle is defined in the interval $v \in [0, v_{max}]$, where v_{max} is the limit speed of the road. Acceleration or speed reduction is always done in the order of 1 cell per unit time, i.e. 1 c/t is accelerated or reduced.

The track is defined by a one-dimensional mesh, or two-dimensional if it is a multi-lane model. The CAs are governed by deterministic or probabilistic rules, with each cell in the mesh having two possible states: empty or occupied, where the cell can only be occupied by a single vehicle at each time step. Depending on the discretization of the problem, a vehicle can be represented by more than one cell.

Wolfram's rule 184 was a pioneer in the modeling of TAC. It describes a one-dimensional CA that considers an occupied black cell and an empty white cell, being a deterministic model. [10,24]

The model proposed by Nagel-Schreckenberg (NaSch) in 1992 was the first to use probabilistic cellular automata. Based on this model, several authors have proposed changes to the rules to better represent the behavior of real traffic. [16, 18]

In general, the models use cell sizes of 7.5 meters, but more refined discretizations are also used to smooth out the simulation. This cell size takes into account the average size a vehicle occupies on a road plus a safety distance from the vehicle in front of it.

The neighborhood N consists of the vehicle immediately in front of you, considering the one-dimensional model. In the multi-lane model, in addition to the vehicle in front, the

2.2. CELLULAR AUTOMATON APPLIED TO TRAFFIC VEHICLE

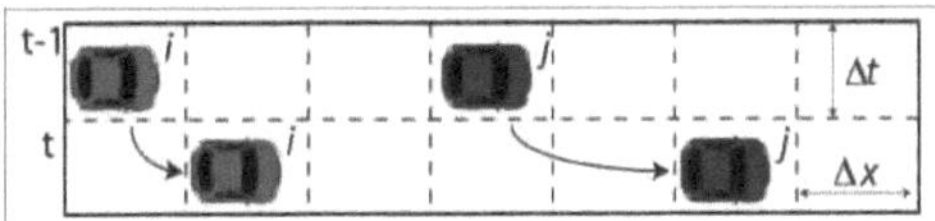

Figura 2.6:   Vehicle Cellular Automaton Model. [24]

Positions in the immediate lanes are also monitored for possible lane changes.

The speed v_i is given in cells per second. Therefore, if vehicle i is traveling at a speed $v_i = 1$ cell/(unit of time), this means that its speed is 7.5m/s or 27km/h. Works that adopt this spatial discretization also usually set the speed limit at 5c/s (cells/second) or 135km/h. Figure 2.6 shows a road with two time instants (t - 1 and t), the discretization is $\Delta = 7.5$m and $\Delta = 1$s. Vehicle i moved at 1c/s, while vehicle j moved at 2c/s. [15,24]

For the simulation, a closed lane is used. All vehicles that reach the end of the lane will return to the beginning, thus creating a periodic contour condition. Therefore, if the lane is of size L, every vehicle that passes this position will return to position xi % L. This modulo operation creates the impression of an infinite lane.

The vehicle's new position at time t is defined by:

$$x_i^t = x_i^{t-1} + v_i \tag{2.2}$$

The rules that describe the behavior of a TAC model consider that all vehicles will accelerate until they reach the maximum speed of the road. To do this, each driver will accelerate their vehicle according to their traffic behavior pattern. In the case of lane change rules, vehicles always look for the lane that has space for the vehicle to reach the maximum speed.

2.3 Concepts of Traffic Flow Theory

The behavior of vehicular traffic is analyzed based on a set of variables: speed (v), density (ρ) and flow (J). It is possible to obtain these variables in two ways: one is static, where at a given moment a "photograph" of the road is taken and the characteristics of the traffic at that specific moment are evaluated, or the other is where a meter is created at some point on the road, which at each time step records the data of the vehicles passing by. [24]

All these measurements are taken over a given period of time, i.e. at each specific time, the data is grouped together and the results recorded. This means that a point on the road is fixed and, over a period of time, the number of cars passing by, those stopped at the point and their respective speeds are recorded. At the end of this period of time, the measurements are calculated and stored for evaluation.

The average speed of the vehicles is given by the arithmetic mean of the speed of each car that passed the meter in a given period of time, according to equation 2.3, where n is the number of vehicles that are on section L of the track, and the sum comprises the sum of the speeds of the cars that were recorded.

$$v = \frac{\sum_{i=1}^{n} v_i}{n} \tag{2.3}$$

9

The flow is the number of vehicles passing the meter in a given period of time. It is calculated according to equation 2.4, where T is the time in seconds that the data was captured, and n is the number of cars.

$$J = \frac{n}{T} \tag{2.4}$$

Density can be obtained by using the number of cars in relation to the size of the roadway, as shown in equation 2.5, where L represents the size of a section of roadway where the data was captured and n the number of cars.

Figura 2.7:   Time interval (h) and space (s) between two vehicles. [24]

$$\rho = \frac{n}{L} \tag{2.5}$$

The vehicular movement data calculated by the above equations can be obtained in two ways: the first considers a section of road of length L at a single moment in time, like a photograph. In this representation, Equations 2.3 and 2.5 describe the density and average speed considering this section of road, of length L.

With these three measures, it is possible to identify different states of traffic on the road, where the quality of its use can be ascertained, under certain conditions and at all road occupancy rates.

In addition to these variables, two other variables are also used in vehicular traffic: spacing (s), which represents the distance between two consecutive vehicles measured from bumper to bumper, as shown in Figure 2.7. The time interval h, is given by the time measured between two consecutive vehicles passing the same observation point, as seen in Figure 2.8 [24].

2.7.1 Stationary State

The stationary state of traffic means, by definition, that all vehicles are moving at the same speed and are equally spaced from each other. It is therefore possible to derive some relationships between the variables involved.

Due to the stationary state of traffic, the time interval (T) in Equation 2.4 can be replaced by the sum of the times (h_i) spent by the vehicles passing a fixed observation point on the road (Equation 2.6), as illustrated in Figure 2.8, where v_i represents the trajectory of vehicle i passing through a point

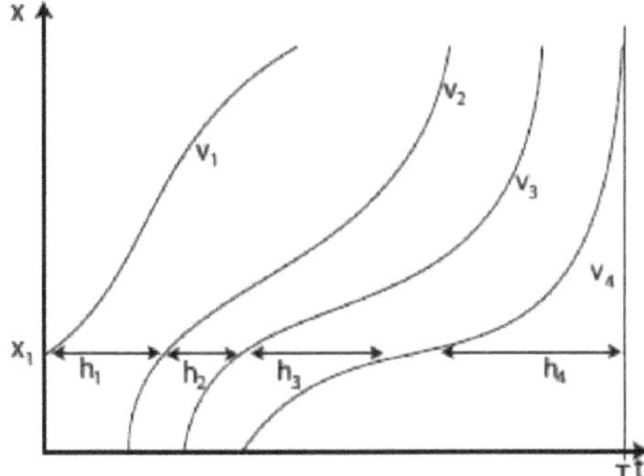

Figura 2.8:   Average time interval. [24]

fixed observation defined as x_i, during a time interval T.

$$J = \frac{n}{\sum_{i=1}^{n} h_i} \tag{2.6}$$

Rewriting Equation 2.6 as a function of the sum of the times, we have:

$$\sum_{i=1}^{n} h_i = \frac{n}{J} \tag{2.7}$$

Dividing both sides of Equation 2.7 by the number of vehicles *(n)* gives the average time interval (h°), which identifies the time between the passage of two vehicles, given that they are in a stationary state.

$$h' = \frac{1}{J} \tag{2.8}$$

Another relationship for density is analogous to Equation 2.5, since L can be rewritten as a function of the sum of the spaces between vehicles passing a fixed observation point, as shown in Equation 2.9 and illustrated in Figure 2.9.

$$\rho = \frac{n}{\sum_{t=1}^{n} s_t} \tag{2.9}$$

11

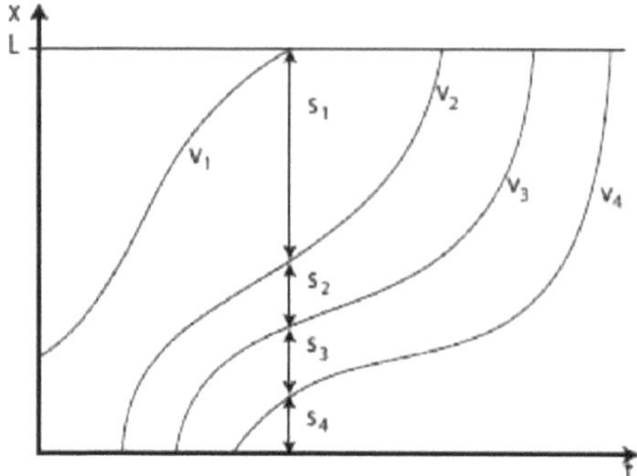

Figure 2.9: Spacing between vehicles. [24]

Rewriting Equation 2.9 in terms of the sums of the spacings gives us:

$$\sum_{t=1}^{n} s_t = \frac{n}{\rho} \tag{2.10}$$

Therefore, the average spacing between vehicles is reached when both sides of Equation 2.10 are divided by the number of vehicles n, resulting in Equation 2.11.

$$s' = \frac{1}{\rho} \tag{2.11}$$

Therefore, considering the fact that the vehicles are moving in a stationary state, it is possible to determine the next position of each vehicle by: $s = v_\circ \times h_\circ$, where $v_\circ$ is the average speed of the road and, in the same way as the other two variables, the speed of each vehicle i *is* equal to the average speed. Therefore, the following relationship can be obtained:

$$v' = \frac{s'}{h'} = \frac{\frac{1}{\rho}}{\frac{1}{J}} = \frac{J}{\rho} \tag{2.12}$$

Finally, a linear relationship is obtained between the three main variables that describe road flow, i.e:

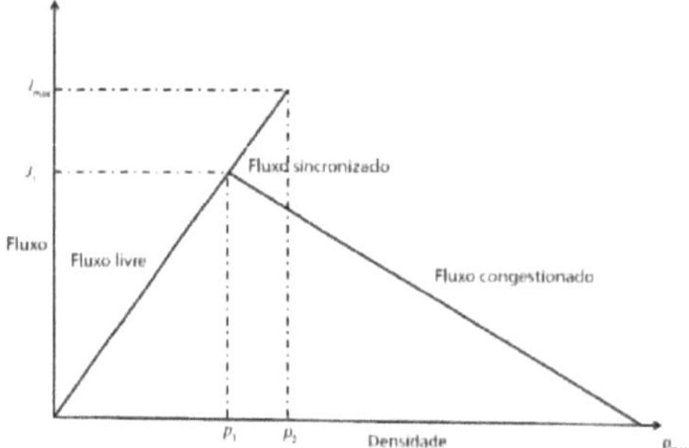

Figure 2.10: Theoretical model of the flow-density diagram. [24]

$$J = \rho v' \qquad (2.13)$$

2.3.2 Traffic Flow Phases

Traffic behavior is described by the result obtained in the previous equations, considering the vehicles over a period of time at a fixed observation point. The diagrams typically used to analyze road flow are: flow-density, density-speed and flow-speed. The space-time diagram can also be used to analyze traffic. [24]

Figure 2.10 shows the theoretical model of the flow-density diagram. In the diagram, three flow phases are well defined as: free, synchronized and congested flow [15], described as:

- Free flow: in this phase there is no interaction between vehicles and they all travel at the desired speed, which is the maximum speed of the lane, and is also the average speed of the lane. It comprises a region of low and medium density ($0 \leq \rho \leq \rho 1$). In this range, the flow increases linearly with increasing density within the interval $0 \leq J \leq J_1$.

- Synchronized flow: this phase comprises a region with medium and high den- sity ($\rho_1 \leq \rho \leq \rho_2$) and maximum flow is reached at J_{max}. However, the flow is also influenced by the interaction between the vehicles and not just by density and speed. As a result, the flow can be free and congested at different times. In free flow, flow is defined in the $J_1 \leq J \leq J_{max}$ range and continues to be characterized by the linear relationship between density and average road speed. As the flow increases in this lane ($J_1 \leq J \leq J_{max}$) and the average speed is kept close to the maximum, the average spacing (s') between vehicles decreases. Although this state shows free flow, the s' is small enough that any fluctuation in speed will end up causing a rapid reduction in the average speed of the road, creating congestion points, making the flow go from free to congested. The vehicles then start to return to the speed they were at, i.e. the speed of the road and the congestion formed are dissolved and the flow goes up to $J = 1$. This process of resuming speed is slow, compared to deceleration, because it happens due to the inertia of the driver's behavior in accelerating. This dynamic ends up giving rise to the region known in the literature as the meta-stability region. [15]

- Congested flow: In congested flow there is an increase in density which causes a reduction in flow. It is a region defined by the density within the range ($\rho 2 \leq \rho \leq \rho max$). In this phase, the congestion formed is not dissolved and moves in the opposite direction to the flow, because as vehicles leave the congestion, others arrive, causing the congestion to move in the opposite direction to the flow.

Figure 2.11 shows the relationship between flow and speed, where you can see that v' is the average speed of the road, which remains just below the maximum speed and the flow is defined as free, remaining free until it reaches the maximum flow (J_{max}), where the optimum speed is obtained (v_o). From this point on, the flow drops and the average speed is also reduced, generating a congested flow.

The diagram illustrated in Figure 2.12 shows the relationship between density and speed, where the average speed of the road is reduced as a result of its saturation.

It is worth noting that when defining the average spacing of vehicles, it is necessary to take into-

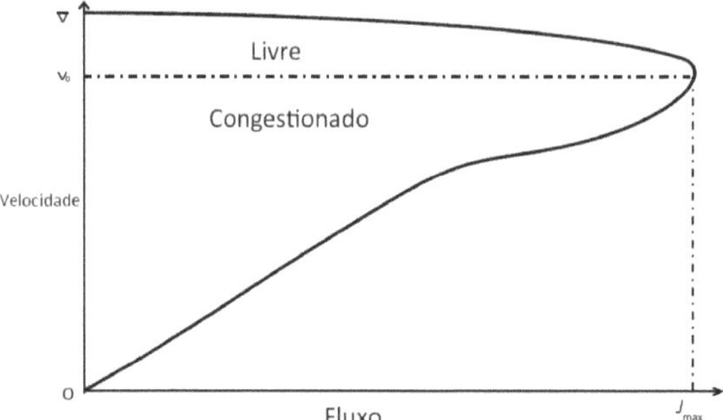

Figure 2.11: Theoretical model of the flow-velocity diagram. [24]

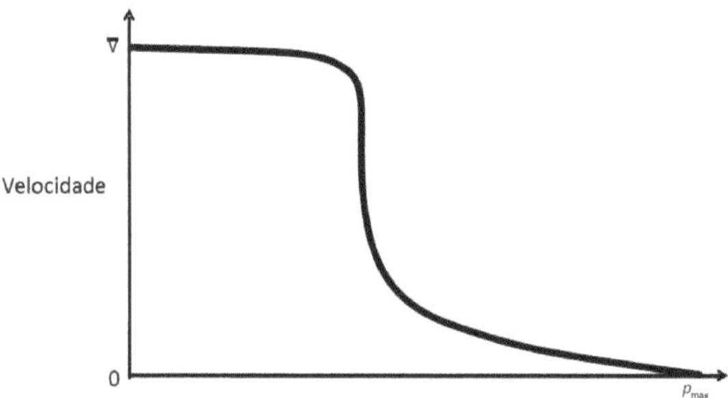

Figure 2.12: Theoretical model of the density-velocity diagram. [24]

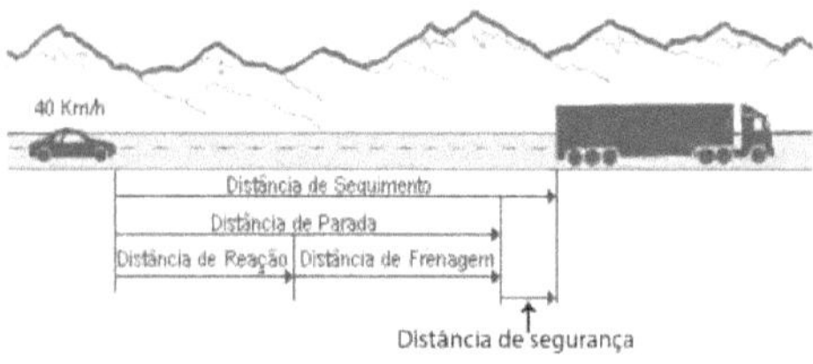

Figure 2.13: Safety distance. [24]

It is essential that there is a distance between two vehicles that allows a vehicle to stop without colliding with the vehicle in front of it. This average spacing distance between vehicles is a function of the driver's reaction time, the space required for him to stop his vehicle, plus a safety distance, as can be seen in Figure 2.13. This distance is calculated according to the speed of the vehicles and, in real cases, also depends on road conditions, weather, etc. [24]

Therefore, for vehicles that have the same safety distance, i.e. a fixed safety distance for all vehicles on the road, it is possible to say that the flow remains free for a higher density value when the maximum speed of the road is lower.

However, the above analysis is only valid as long as the linear relationship is sustained by the average speed of the road being equal to the maximum speed. It is known that from a certain point onwards, vehicles cannot travel at their maximum speed and have to reduce it, depending on the distance they are from the vehicle in front of them. Therefore, different flow values can be obtained by combining the different distances between vehicles and the different speeds that these vehicles may be moving in the congested flow, since it is known that the density of the road can be expressed as a function of the spacing between vehicles.

Chapter 3

Cellular Automata on GPU

Given the logical structure of CA, where the same calculation is performed on different pieces of information, which are not dependent on each time step, the SIMD architecture provides an environment that optimizes computation for problems with this structure, an architecture found in GPUs. In order to evaluate the parallelization of CA on these architectures, a CUDA implementation of the Gol application was proposed. Given the results, it is believed that good performance can also be obtained with TAC. [2, 4, 7, 19, 20]

3.1 GPU Computing

The demand for computing power, the growing processing capacity of GPUs, with special attention to the new generation and the low cost of this hardware, have made the use of GPUs in supercomputers more common. Currently, most supercomputers are equipped with some form of GPU. On the other hand, without as much processing power compared to a GPU, there are the CPUs that make up these large supercomputer systems. Although they have greater processing capacity, as shown in Figure 3.1, GPUs are not capable of processing any type of problem or running any operating system. In this way, CPUs are still required both for managing GPUs and for processing applications with the following characteristics

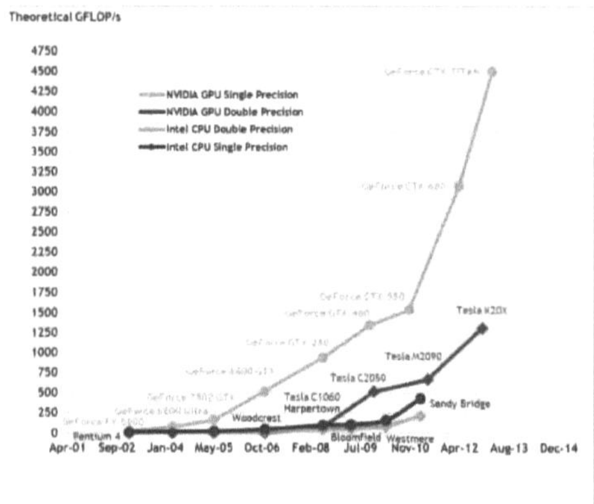

Figure 3.1: Comparison of processing power between GPU and CPU.

MIMD (Multiple Instructions Multiple Data), which are used in more generic problems, as they need to execute multiple instructions on different data. [8,14,20]

Currently, high-performance GPU programming relies on two languages: OpenCL and CUDA. OpenCL (Open Computer Language) is a set of APIs that allow you to work with GPUs from intel, nVidia and ATI, as well as multicore processors. The CUDA language is nVidia's own, is available free of charge and was the first to allow applications to be developed in a higher-level language compared to shader languages. Since

16

then, work in the field of GPU parallel processing has started to consider the GPU as a cluster, i.e. a single graphics card has been defined as a cluster.

In addition, the CUDA language is evolving more quickly than the OpenCL language and has features not yet implemented in OpenCL, such as virtual memory and power control, done through the clock of the cores and access to GPU memory. [20]

Graphics cards (or GPUs) are specific units for image processing. However, for some time now they have been used to perform calculations that require a great deal of computational effort. By promoting a parallel environment on a single circuit board, the architecture provides a great deal of processing power at a relatively low cost.

Each GPU allows the use of millions of processing threads. This structure is exemplified in Figure 3.2, where you can see the division of the logical structures into kernel, grid, block and thread components. All the threads in a block share local memory, and all the threads on the board share global memory, where the information is copied at the start of the computation. Within the GPU memory hierarchy, other specific memories are present to better serve graphics applications, as seen in Figure 3.3 [8,14,20].

CUDA has 6 different types of memory as seen in .3. Each thread has its own local memory, which are the variables declared inside the kernel, and registers, which have the same function as the CPU registers and are not defined by the programmer. Each block has a memory called shared memory, because the same information is available to all the threads in that block. There is also global memory, constant memory and texture memory. The latter two are read-only and the texture memory has an automatic cache.

While local memory, shared memory and constant memory are extremely fast to access (around 4 flops), global memory and texture memory are very slow (around 700 flops). For this reason, it is common at the start of processing to move the most accessed parts of the global memory to the shared memory and then execute the algorithm. The developer must plan his solution carefully, grouping threads that act in equivalent or close memory positions into blocks. As you can see, performance can vary greatly.

This type of hardware provides developers with a SIMD (Single Instruction Multiple Data) architecture, meaning that the same instruction is executed on different data. A new nomenclature for this architecture, which has been more widely adopted due to the use of GPUs, is SIMT (Single Instruction Multiple Threads).

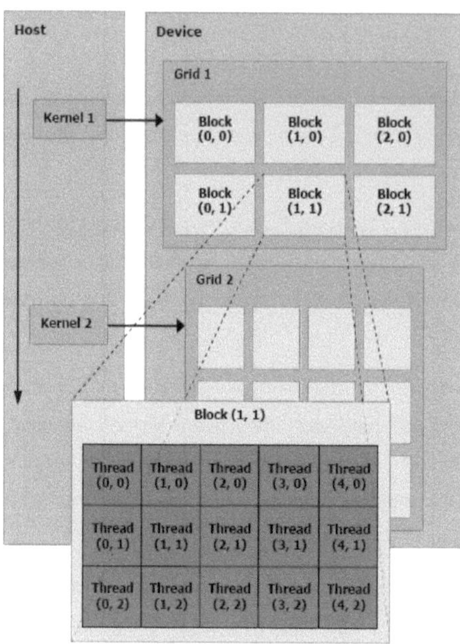

Figure 3.2: Division model of the GPU logic structure. [20]

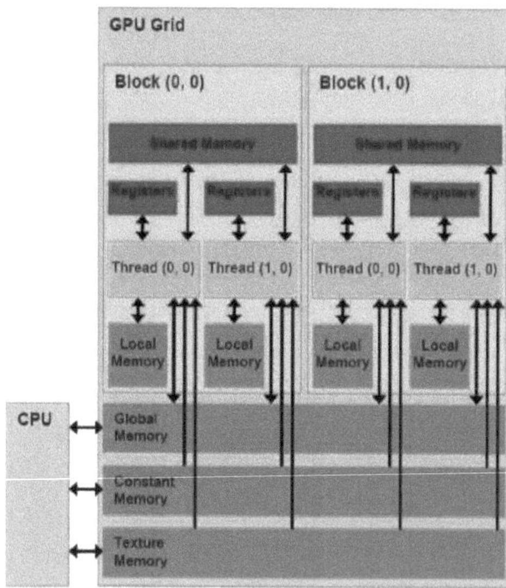

Figure 3.3: Memory hierarchy in CUDA. [20]

It differs in that the threads modify the data, which is a more appropriate idea for the plaid architecture, since the same instruction is executed in each thread, which is responsible for obtaining the data destined for it.

[7,12]

With the use of GPUs, a major problem that existed until then has been eliminated, as seen in Figure 3.4. It is often the case that a small part of the code is responsible for most of the computational effort. As this division is not harmonious, the superior number of processors in GPUs benefits and encourages their use for data-independent calculations that can be parallelized in some way.

Graphics cards have been developed to serve as a co-processor, i.e. an auxiliary processor to the CPU (Central Processor Unit). Their use is therefore conditional on integration with CPU programming. Therefore, the integration of parallelization in the two layers would provide better results compared to using them separately. [19]

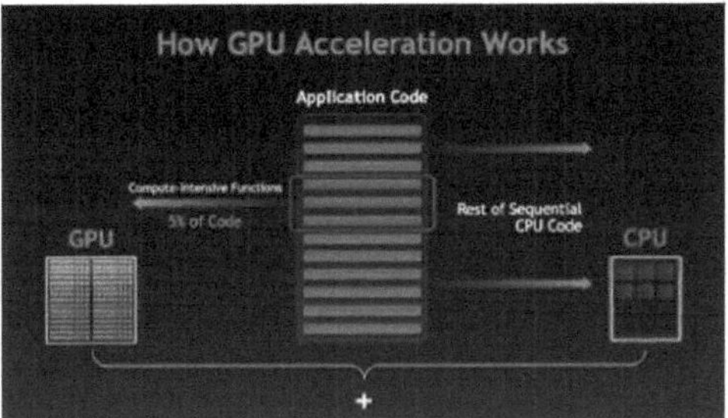

Figure 3.4: Processing Division.

3.2 Expected improvement

For the GOL problem, the expected improvement is based on parallelizing the step of calculating and updating the matrix, which represents the mesh of cells. The previous time is shown in Equation 3.1, where m and n are the dimensions of the matrix and t is the number of generations, or time steps, and u is the unit of time needed to calculate and update the state of each cell. After parallelization, the time is reduced as seen in Equation 3.2, because all the cells will have their states updated in one unit of time, and it remains to multiply this time by the number of generations required.

$$tempo_{sequencial} = ((m * n) * u) * t \tag{3.1}$$

$$tempo_{paralelo} = u * t \tag{3.2}$$

In the sequential implementation of TAC, to calculate the information for a TAC scenario, with a single lane of c cells or c * 7.5m, with occupancy of n vehicles, and generating t time steps, each time step is equivalent to 1 second. Taking the time to calculate the state changes of each vehicle as u, the total processing time is expressed in Equation 3.3. However, with the parallelized code, it is reduced according to Equation 3.2, not taking into account the details of the implementation and architecture, where the following is considered

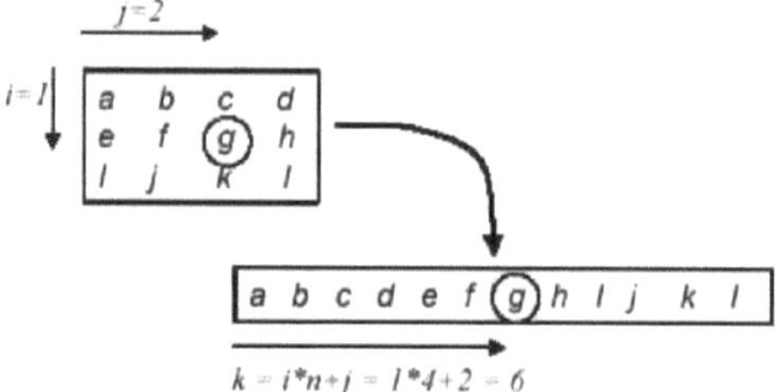

Figure 3.5: Transforming a matrix into a vector.

which has a number of threads greater than or equal to the number of vehicles. In this approach, each thread is responsible for calculating the state transition of each vehicle.

$$tempo_{sequencial} = (n * u) * t \qquad (3.3)$$

Some details are necessary for this integration between coprocessor and processor, one of which is the passing of information between the two processing structures. One of the main differences that interfere with programming a CA using CUDA is the passing of matrices, since CUDA does not recognize this structure. For a matrix to be passed to the GPU, it must be converted into vector format. In this format, the calculations are carried out on the co-processor and, after returning, a new transformation must be carried out in order to have data that conforms to the CA model used, .5 [20].

It's worth noting that parallelization with the CUDA language has some drawbacks, such as the copying of memory, which in some cases is detrimental to the overall performance of the application. This *overhead* becomes clear when the amount of computation allocated to the GPU is relatively small. Therefore, the time spent copying memory can exceed the computation time, making the use of the GPU inadvisable.

3.3 GOL parallelization methodology

The structure created for the GOL simulation is based on two matrices, the main one holding the state of the cells at the current moment in time, and the temporary matrix holding the information for updating the state of the cells. After initialization, the two matrices are copied to the GPU's global memory. Subsequently, the generation loop is created and, within this loop, a call is made to the   function is called   , which is responsible for calculating the changes of

state of the cells. When the function executed on the Device finishes, all the threads are synchronized and the information contained in the temporary matrix is copied to the main matrix. As a result, all the matrices have up-to-date data on their neighborhood. At the end of the loop, the matrices are copied back into the Host's memory and the result is displayed.

GPUs have several memory structures, the only one used being global memory, and tests have shown that the use of shared memories and registers has not resulted in any benefit, even causing a worsening in performance. These peculiarities can be caused by the structure of the calculation, where there is a lot of access to memory and little computation. Remember that data always needs to pass through main memory, then be copied to other memory structures and finally accessed. As a result, the overhead of copying data from global memory and vice versa is detrimental to performance, rather than beneficial.

3.4 Proposed methodology for parallelizing the TAC

Like all CAs, the TAC is discretized in time, i.e. the states of all the cars are calculated at time t, where each thread created on the GPU calculates the state changes of each vehicle. At the end of this time step, all the threads are synchronized and the information unified. As a result, in the next time step, all vehicles have up-to-date information on their immediate surroundings.

The structuring of the implementation can directly affect the application's performance. Therefore, a better division of processing, as well as a better structuring of the implementation, was sought in order to improve the application's performance.

For the part of the code that is executed on the CPU, we used the C programming language, which is very widespread and easy to maintain. The CUDA language is based on the C language, so the two are very compatible. [20]

After initializing the application variables, a repetition structure was set up. To reproduce the interaction in the amount of lane occupancy, information is calculated from 1% occupancy to 99% lane occupancy, to better evaluate the system. From this point on, the implementation is aimed at modeling the lanes together with the vehicles.

At this point we have a loop in time, within which the parallelization is carried out. A function is created with the TAC code, i.e. the logic that moves the vehicles in the lanes. The definition __global__ is placed before the function, this identifies that the function is called by the *Host* (CPU) and will be executed on the Device (GPU). Along with calling the function, it is necessary to allocate and copy the data from the *Host* memory to the *Device*. As in the previous case, it is necessary to use a temporary array to store the information to be updated. In the TAC model, each vehicle has various pieces of information, such as position, size, speed in x and y. This information needs to be copied into the *Device*'s memory along with the track information.

Functions within the TAC code are subdivided to create clearer and cleaner code, using the __device__ tag, which are functions called within the *Device* and will also be executed on the *Device*. After the generation *loop* has finished, the information is returned to the Host's memory and the data on flow, density and average speed is recorded in *log* files for later analysis.

Chapter 4

Case Studies

CAs allow the modeling of many problems. In view of this, some tests were carried out to validate the improvement in performance when using parallel computing on GPUs.

4.1 Game of Life

The GoL model is characterized by being theoretical, i.e. it does not aim to obtain a practical result for a real-world problem. Therefore, the objective of the implementation is based on the correct computation of the steps until the end of the simulation. With this in mind and based on the literature, the sequential model was implemented with a simple logic and easy coding. [10,21]

Algorithm 1 presents the main part of the Goal logic. The complete code can be seen in Appendix A. Its logic is simple and easy to code, with just three nested *loops* and a few queries to the positions in the matrix to get the result of each cell.

In Algorithm 1, the first loop is responsible for iterating over time, and the two inner loops navigate through all the cells in the matrix. The matrix is filled with zeros and ones, where zero represents a dead cell and one, a live cell, so the neighboring cells are accessed if the neighboring cell

---

Algorithm 1 Partial GoL Pseudo-Code

1:    **for** i $\leftarrow$ 0 **until** it generates **do**

2:    **for** j $\leftarrow$ 0 **until** tam **do**

3:    **for** k $\leftarrow$ 0 **until** tam **do**

4:    *cont* $\leftarrow$ 0

5:    *cont* $\leftarrow$ *mesh[abs((j* + 1)%tam)][abs((k - 1)%tam)]*

6:    *cont* $\leftarrow$ *mesh[abs(j%tam)][abs((k - 1)%tam)]*

7:    *cont* $\leftarrow$ *mesh[abs((j - 1)%tam)][abs((k - 1)%tam)]*

8:    *cont* $\leftarrow$*mesh[abs((j*+ 1)%tam)][abs(k%tam)]*

9:    *cont* $\leftarrow$ *mesh[abs((j - 1')%tam)][abs(k%tam)]*

10: *cont* $\leftarrow$*mesh[abs((j*+ 1')%tam)][abs((k + 1)%tam)]*

11: *cont* $\leftarrow$ *mesh[abs(j%tam)][abs((k + 1)%tam)]*

12: *cont* $\leftarrow$ *mesh[abs((j - 1')%tam)][abs((k + 1)%tam)]*

13: **if** *cont* < 2 AND *mesh[j]*[k] == 1 **then**

14:     *malhatT emp[j][k]* = 0

15:   **else if** *cont* == 3 AND *mesh[j][k]* == 0 **then**

16:     *meshT emp[j][k]* = 0

17:   **else if** *cont* >= 2 AND *cont* <= 3 AND *mesh[j][k]* == 1 **then**

18:     *meshT emp[j][k]* = 1

19:   **else if** *cont* > 3 AND *mesh[j][k]* == 1 **then**

20:     *meshT emp[j][k]* = 0

21:   **end if**

22:   **end to**

23:   **end to**

24:   **At the end of the process**, the counter is increased by one. Then the GoL rules are applied, and at the end we have an auxiliary matrix with the new states of the cells, so this information is copied to the main matrix and the process repeated several times.

The model has no data visualization, only a terminal representation, as follows: where there is a live cell, the position of the matrix is displayed with an "*" and when the cell is dead, the position is empty. After validating the implementation, which was based on entering a known structure and checking its evolution, it was modified so that its computing core is processed in parallel with the CUDA language.

Chapter 5

Results and Discussion

To evaluate the proposal, the following environment was used: Intel Core i7 3770 processor, clocked at 3.4GHz, 8mb of cache memory and 12Gb of RAM at 1333MHz, 2 NVIDIA GT 640 video cards, Ubuntu 12.04, CUDA 6. Tests were also carried out with a GTX 570 video card, to get an idea of the difference between low-cost and high-performance cards. It was installed in a computer with the following configuration: Intel Core i7 950 processor, clocked at 3.07GHz, 8mb of cache memory and 12Gb of RAM at 1600MHz, 1 NVIDIA GTX 570 video card, Ubuntu 12.04, CUDA 6.

The results presented were calculated by taking the average of five consecutive timings. The times of the implementations were obtained using the clock() function of the C language, which measures the time of the entire implementation and, in the parallel implementation, cudaEventRecord() was used. The operating system was set to text mode and no other processes were initialized. Only one video card was used, *Device* 1, because by *default,* the OS sends the images to *Device* 0. *Device* 1 therefore receives no workload and is free for the calculations of the processes assigned to it, which does not interfere with the times obtained.

The results obtained are divided into two parts, the first referring to the case study in which the Gol problem was implemented to validate the improvement.

that a CA would have on its performance, with the use of parallelization with CUDA. Speed-up was used as a measure of comparison between sequential and parallel execution times. [11]

5.1 Goal Results

In the Gol application, it was observed that the parallel time, in relation to the square matrix of size 10, is worse than the sequential one, as shown in Table 1. This is explained by the need to exchange information between the *Host* and *Device.* When the matrix size is increased, the initial communication loss is absorbed by the computation time. As a result, sequential performance is easily exceeded.

You can see that as the size of the simulated model increases, the computation time grows linearly. As with parallel code, there is a limit to the parallelization of the structure used, because at each iteration, all the *threads* need to be synchronized. It can be seen that the *speed - up* is stabilized at around 3.5. This limit is reached due to the nature of the problem, which requires data to be synchronized at each time step.

Based on these results, new tests were carried out with the aim of improving this performance ratio. However, even with the use of memories with shorter access times, the overall time remained the same. This peculiarity can be explained by the *overhead* in the exchange of context between *Host* and *Device*, and the improvement in performance was nullified by the *overhead*. The shared memories and registers were tested, with the register being assigned to the *cont* variable, as seen in Code 3.1, and the shared memory receiving the input matrix from the global memory.

Matrix size	Simulation steps	Sequential time (ms)	Paratelo time (ms)	Speed-up
10	1000	10,000	21,207	0,4715
IOO	1000	480,000	170,221	2,8198
1000	1000	48.260.000,000	13.474.863,281	3,5814
2000	1000	192.430.000,000	53.914.535,156	3,5691
5000	1000	1.199.970.000,000	336.979.875,000	3,5609
8000	1000	3.072.020.000,000	864.370.187,500	3,5540
10000	1000	4.800.080.000,000	1.352.506.500,000	3,5490

Table 5.1: Goal results

5.2 TAC results

Based on the tests and results obtained, it is believed that good performance can also be achieved by TAC. The possibilities for improvement are more obvious, as the logic is more complex, with more computation and more data distributed to each *thread*.

The results described in Tables 5.2, 5.3, 5.4 and 5.5 show the comparison between the sequential time and the parallel times achieved on the two graphics cards in relation to the TAC. Two *speed-ups* are obtained, one for the GT 640 and the other for the GTX 570. The following tables do not have the instance of 1024000 cars for the GTX 570 card, as it presented errors during the run.

However, the same problem presented by the GTX 570 was also noticed when running with the GT 640 GPU, when Device 0 was used, which is set by the OS as the default video output. This means that sharing the GPU with the OS display can compromise the results. As such, the errors presented in the last instance run by the GTX 570 cannot be accurately determined.

Table 5.2 shows that there is no improvement in performance when using the GT 640. However, the GTX 570 achieves an improvement, but it is not maintained. The data shown in Figures 5.1, 5.2, 5.3, 5.4 and 5.5 also show that, under the conditions described in Table 5.2, there is a lot of memory usage and the computing time is minimal in relation to the whole. As a result, the use of GPUs for small problems does not prove to be effective.

Table 5.3 shows a significant improvement, both with the GT 640 GPU and the GTX 570. It is also worth noting the gap between the results of the GPUs, where the GTX 570 is already at least 5 times faster than the GT 640.

In Table 5.4, the results of the 3-hour simulation again show increasing *speed-up* values for the GTX 570 card, but the results for the GT 640 begin to stabilize.

With the 24-hour simulation (Table 5.5), it can again be seen that the results obtained with the GT 640 show an improvement, but are not very different from the sequential simulation run. However, the use of the GTX 570 card achieves the maximum improvement, reaching a speed - *up* of 95.

Quantity Cars	Time of Simulation	Sequential time (ms)	Parallel Time (ms) (GT640)	Speed-up in relation to to the GT640	Parallel Time (ms) (GTX570)	Speed-up in relation to the GTX570
1024	1	0,079	1.807.000	4,37189E-08	0,046	1,717391304
2048	1	0,158	2.897.000	5,45392E-08	0,058	2,724137931
10240	1	0,306	13.013.000	2,35149E-08	1.214.000	2,52059E-07
20480	1	0,11	29.603.001	3,71584E-09	2.220.000	4,95495E-08
102400	1	3.845.000	250.828.018	0,015329228	34.787.003	0,110529786
204800	1	6.445.000	709.734.985	0,009080854	104.369.003	0,061752051
1024000	1	32.282.001	40.675.082.031	0,000793655		

Table 5.2: 1-second TAC results

Quantity Cars	Time of Simulation	Sequential time (ms)	Parallel Time (ms) (GT640)	Speed-up in relation to to the GT640	Parallel Time (ms) (GTX570)	Speed-up in relation to the GTX570
1024	1000	35.445.004	26.702.002	1,327428707	12.395.000	2,859621138
2048	1000	68.773.003	38.443.970	1,788915219	12.876.000	5,341177617
10240	1000	313.489.014	128.710.999	2,435603922	30.331.001	10,33559736
20480	1000	618.833.984	249.266.006	2,482624863	55.249.004	11,20081701
102400	1000	3.243.262.939	1.096.303.955	2,958361068	320.864.000	10,10790534
204800	1000	6.491.431.152	2.368.689.941	2,740515354	618.336.975	10,49820958
1024000	1000	32.467.912.109	49.088.019.531	0,661422327		

Table 5.3: TAC results 1000 seconds

Quantity Cars	Time of Simulation	Sequential time (ms)	Parallel Time (ms) (GT640)	Speed-up in relation to to the GT640	Parallel Time (ms) (GTX570)	Speed-up in relation to the GTX570
1024	3600	132.547.012	92.808.006	1,428185107	44.238.003	2,996225033
2048	3600	257.733.948	130.791.000	1,970578618	45.894.001	5,615852669
10240	3600	1.156.977.051	429.901.031	2,691263727	107.849.007	10,72774876
20480	3600	2.294.601.074	823.192.017	2,787443302	158.526.530	14,47455561
102400	3600	11.707.122.070	3.293.745.117	3,554349731	583.218.018	20,07332028
204800	3600	23.360.326.172	6.708.083.984	3,482414088	653.309.998	35,75687842
1024000	3600	116.350.992.188	71.064.062.500	1,637269079		

Table 5.4: TAC results 3600 seconds

Quantity Cars	Time of Simulation	Sequential time (ms)	Parallel Time (ms) (GT640)	Speed-up in relation to to the GT640	Parallel Time (ms) (GTX570)	Speed-up in relation to the GTX570
1024	10800	427.124.023	278.591.980	1,533152616	135.632.004	3,149138923
2048	10800	828.927.063	395.338.013	2,096755272	135.953.003	6,097158906
10240	10800	3.736.099.121	1.295.138.916	2,88470918	309.671.997	12,06469799
20480	10800	7.111.412.109	2.446.550.049	2,906710252	388.797.028	18,29080882
102400	10800	35.535.105.469	9.443.130.859	3,763063967	705.286.987	50,38389496
204800	10800	70.473.406.250	18.764.396.484	3,755697995	739.443.970	95,30594488
1024000	10800	348.614.781.250	131.946.984.375	2,642082219		

Table 5.5: TAC results 10800 seconds

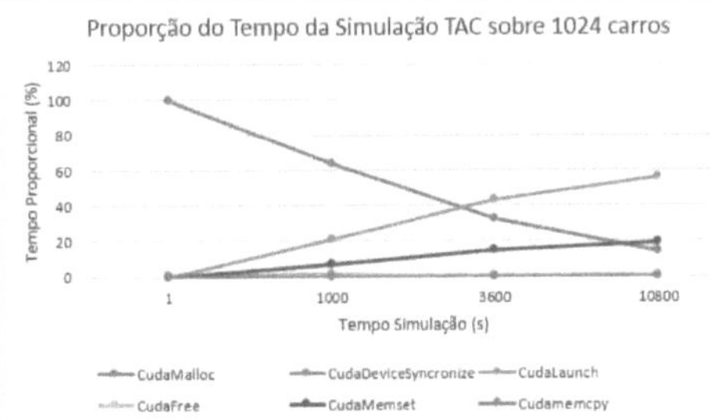

Figura 5.1:   Proportion of TAC simulation time over 1024 cars.

Figures 5.1, 5.2, 5.3, 5.4, 5.5, 5.6 and 5.7 show the results obtained using CUDA's "nvprof" command. This command results in a detailed display of the time spent by each main parallel computing structure. The ratios of CudaMalloc, CudaFree, CudaDeviceSyncronize, Cuda- Memset, CudaLaunch and CudaMemCpy to the total computation time are shown in the figures. They were chosen because they account for most of the time spent computing, as well as providing information on critical operations.

Figure 5.1 shows the results for the simulation of 1024 cars, where all the simulation times are observed. This gives a visualization of which operations take the most and least time, depending on the characteristics of the simulation. It can be seen that, with the execution of a few time steps, the time spent allocating the structures in the Device is very large. As the number of steps increases, the allocation time is absorbed by the execution time (CudaLaunch).

By increasing the number of cars to 2048, you can see that the information remains the same, but the other operations begin to take up larger chunks of time.

In Figure 5.3, you can see that other operations are starting to stand out in terms of execution times. CudaDeviceSyncronize is the time taken to synchronize all the threads, and in this simulation the number of threads was

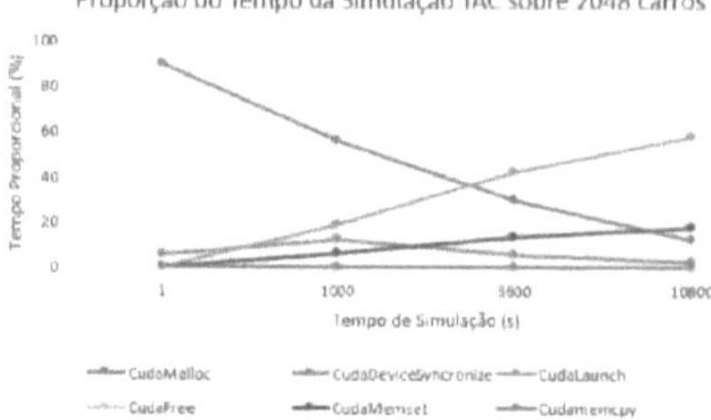

Figura 5.2:   Proportion of TAC simulation time over 1024 cars.

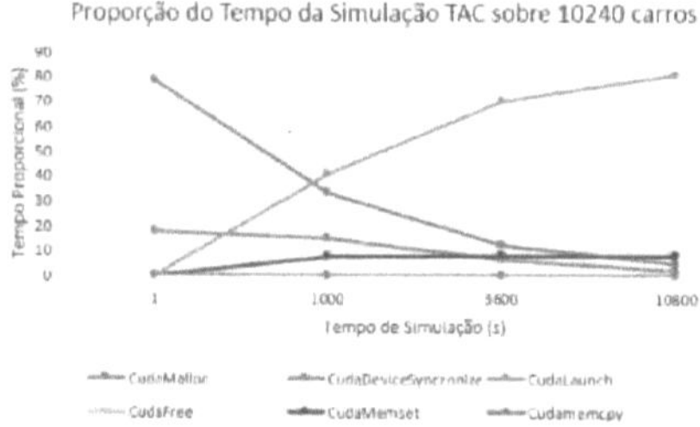

Figura 5.3:   Proportion of TAC simulation time over 10240 cars.

When the number of time steps exceeds 10000, the time spent is high. However, as in the previous figures, in simulations with few time steps, the allocation operation is still the biggest problem with parallelization. As the time steps increase, the execution time takes up almost all of the time spent.

As seen above, Figure 5.4 shows similar results, only with the simulation size changed to 20480.

Figures 5.5 and 5.6 show the simulations with 102400 and 204800 cars respectively. Both show similar data, with thread synchronization beginning to take up more and more of the simulation time when there are only a few steps. As simulation time increases, these operations decrease in proportion to the total time spent, with execution time accounting for almost all of the time spent.

In Figure 5.7, you can see another scenario, where again in the

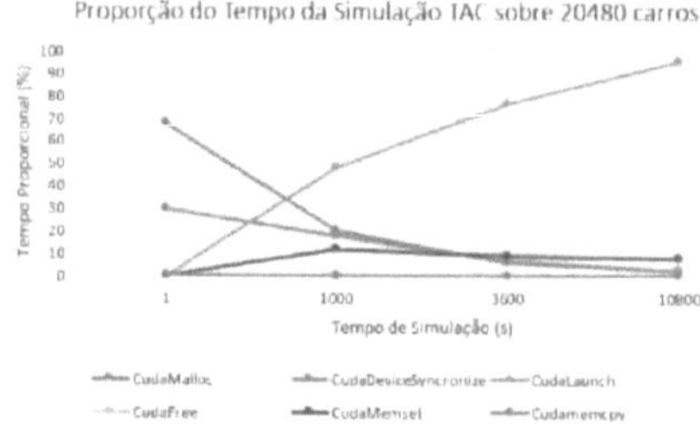

Figura 5.4:   Proportion of TAC simulation time over 20480 cars.

28

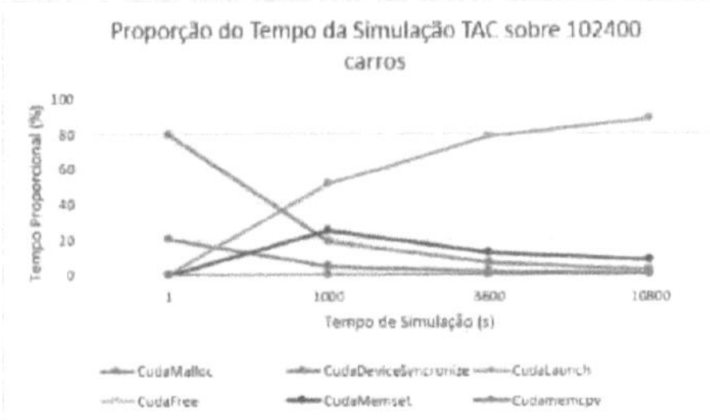

Figura 5.5: Proportion of TAC Simulation Time over 102400 cars.

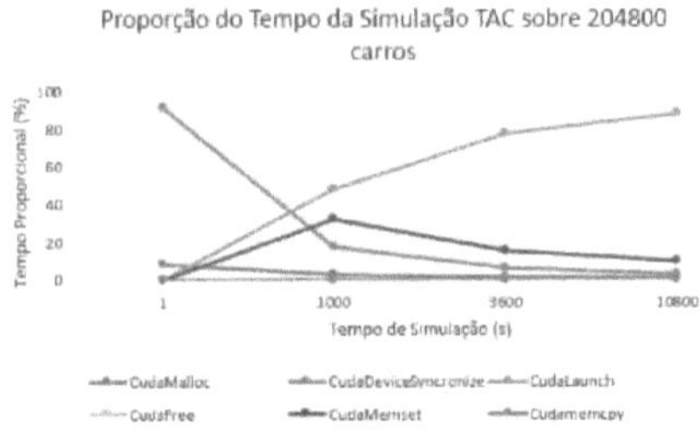

Figura 5.6: Proportion of TAC simulation time over 204800 cars.

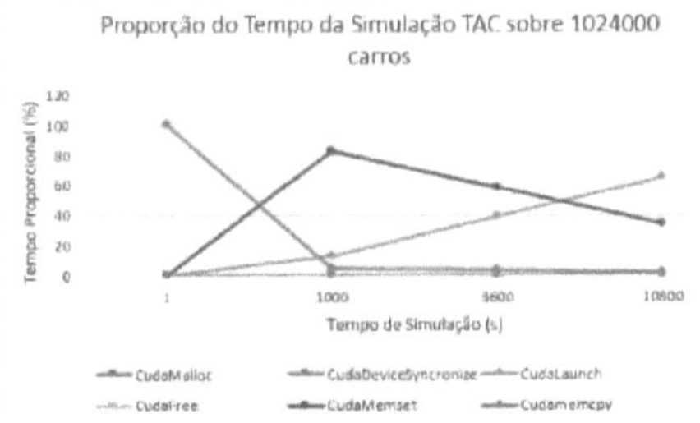

Figura 5.7: Proportion of TAC simulation time over 1024000 cars.

In a 1-second simulation, you can see that a lot of time is spent synchronizing the threads. As the simulation progresses, the time spent begins to be used preferentially for memory operations. Only when the simulation reaches its last instance does the time spent processing outweigh the other operations.

5.3 Discussion

The results of both the case study and the TAC implementation show that parallelization is not suitable for very small problems. This can be justified by the high cost of communication between Host and Device, especially in operations involving allocation and synchronization. Therefore, the results confirm this claim. As the problem domain increases, more threads work simultaneously, reducing processing time compared to sequential code, as well as being filled with more workload, showing a significant improvement over sequential results.

Chapter 6

Conclusion

Taking into account the results obtained, it is possible to state that the models studied and implemented produce satisfactory results.

The data resulting from the parallelization of Gol shows the ability of a CA to improve its performance with the use of CUDA programming, with a speed-up of approximately 3.5. The satisfactory results were obtained using a low-cost, low-performance GPU, which has great potential for improvement over high-performance GPUs.

The model proposed for parallelizing the TAC is close to the model applied to the Gol. As such, it is effective in improving simulation performance. Analyzing the logic of each problem, the TAC is shown to be more conducive to parallelization, as it has a greater number of instructions that would be executed in parallel. With the use of the GTX 570, the speed - up reaches 95, showing a significant improvement.

The results also showed the gap in performance between low-cost and high-performance boards. The maximum difference achieved was 25 times, in the instance of 204800 cars, in a 24-hour simulation.

Taking into account the information obtained, together with data from previous studies, it can be said that the cases discussed have great benefits.

in the use of parallel programming with the CUDA language.

References

[1] BAYS, C. Candidates for the game of life in three dimensions. Complex *Systems 1* (1987), p. 373-400.

[2] BRADAO, D., ZAMITH, M. P. D. M., CLUA, E., MONTENEGRO, A., BULCAO, A., MADEIRA, D., KISCHINHEVSKY, M., and LEAL- TOLEDO, R. C. P. Performance evaluation of optimized implementations of finite difference method for wave propagation problems on gpu architecture. *In (SBACPADW/WAMCA), IEEE* (2010), p. 7-12.

[3] da ROCHA, R., and NETO, J. Adaptive automaton, limits and complexity in comparison with the turing machine. *University of Sao Paulo (USP)* (2000).

[4] da SILVA, A. R., da S. P. MARTINS, C. A., and JÛNIOR, M. M. G. Parallel computational simulation based on cellular automata: A case study in cloud dynamics simulation. *Annals of EATI - Annual Meeting of Information Technology and Academic Week of Information Technology Year 3*, n. 1 (2013), p. 163-171.

[5] de MELOS, M. P. R. Game of life with cuda. *II RAIC XXIV JIC II SEPTI(II Annual Scientific Initiation Meeting XXIV Scientific Initiation Day II Research, Technology and Innovation Week), JFRRJ (Federal Rural University of Rio de Janeiro)* (2014).

[6] de MELOS, M. P. R. Parallelization of cellular automata on graphics cards with cuda. *I ERSI-RJ (I Regional School of Information Systems of Rio de Janeiro), JFF (Fluminense Federal University)* (2014).

[7] EICHENBERGER, A. E., WU, P., and O'BRIEN, K. Vectorization for simd architectures with alignment constraints. IBM T.J. Watson Research Center (2004).

[8] FARBER, R. CUDA: application design and development, 315f. ed. Morgan Kaufman, 2011.

[9] GARDNER, M. Mathematical games - the fantastic combinations of john conway's new solitaire game "life". *Scientific American v. 223* (1970), p. 120123.

[10] GREMONINI, L., and VICENTINI, E. Cellular automata: bibliographical review and examples of implementations. *Revista Eletrônica Lato Sensu - UNICENTRO* (2008).

[11] HENNESSY, J. L., and PATTERSON, D. *Computer Architecture: A quantitative Approach*, 5th ed. ed. Morgan Kaufman, 2011.

[12] JAM, B., MONTRUCCHIO, B., RAGUSA, C., KHAN, F. G., and KHAN, O. Fast parallel sorting algorithms on gpus. *International Journal of Distributed and Parallel Systems (IJDPS) Vol. 3*, No. 6 (November 2012), p. 107-118.

[13] KERNER, B. S., KLENOV, S. L., and SCHRECKENBERG, M. Simple cellular automaton model for traffic breakdown, highway capacity, and synchronized flow. *Journal de Physique Rev. E 84* (Oct 2011).

[14] KIRK, D., and HWU, W. *Programming massively parallel processors: a hands-on approach*, 2sd edition, 496f., ed. Morgan Kaufman, 2013.

[15] LIMA, E., and LEAL-TOLEDO, R. Cellular automata model for multi-lane road traffic with movement anticipation. *In: SBMAC (Sociedade Brasileira de Matemàtica, Estatistica e Computaçao), XXXI CNMAC (XXXI Congresso Nacional de Matemàtica, Estatistica e Computaçao)*, (2008), p. 665-671.

[16] MATEUS, J. Um autòmato celular para tràfego em multifaixas. (87f.) disserta- çào (mestre em matemàtica aplicada). *Department of Applied Mathematics, Faculty of Sciences, University of Porto* (2001).

[17] MORANDA, B., MELO, C., ALBUQUERQUE, J., BOCANEGRA, S., PAREDES, H., SOUZA-SANTOS, R., de SOUZA, M., and BARBOSA, C. Cellular automata applied to the epidemiology of schistosomiasis in pernambuco - a comparative analysis of mollusc collection processes. *In: Proceedings of the XXXI National Congress of Applied and Computational Mathematics. Brazilian Society of Applied and Computational Mathematics;* (2008), p. 630-636.

[18] NAGEL, K., and SCHRECKENBERG, M. A cellular automaton model for freeway traffic. *Journal of Physique I 2* (Dec. 1992), p. 2221-2229.

[19] PHARR, M., and F., R. *GPU gems 2: programming techniques for highper- formance graphics and general-purpose computation.*, ed. ed. Addison-Wesley professional, 2005.

[20] SANDERS, J., and KANDROT, E. *CUDA by Example: an introduction to general-purpose GPU programming*, 290f. ed. Addison-Wesley Professional, 2010.

[21] SCHIFF, J. *Cellular Automata: A discrete View of the World.* Wiley Interscience, 2008.

[22] SOUSA, S. A. F. S. *Autómatos celulares. (96f.) Monografia.* Department of Computer Science, Faculty of Sciences, University of Porto, 2001.

[23] TAVARES, L. (66f). an urban traffic simulator based on cellular automata. dissertation (master's degree in electrical engineering). *Post-Graduation in Electrical Engineering, School of Engineering, Federal University of Minas Gerais* (2010).

[24] ZAMITH, M. P. D. M. (128f). a cellular automaton model applied to road traffic with multiple driver profiles. Thesis *(PhD in Mathematical Modeling)* (2013).

Appendix A

Implementations

The implementations carried out for the work follow.

A.1 Codes

Code A.1: Sequential GoL Code

```c
#include <stdio.h>
#include <stdlib.h>
#include <unistd.h>
#include <time.h>
#include <math.h>

int main(int argc, char *argv[]){

  int tam = atoi(argv[1]);
  int gera = atoi(argv[2]);
  int min = atoi(argv[3]);
  int max = atoi(argv[4]);
  int i, j, k, cont;

  clock_t ini, fim;

  int **malha;
  int **malhaTemp;

  malha = (int**)(malloc(tam*sizeof(int*)));
  malhaTemp = (int**)(malloc(tam*sizeof(int*)));

    for(k = 0; k < tam; k++){
```

```c
    malha[k] = (int*)(malloc(tam*sizeof(int)));
  malhaTemp[k] = (int*)(malloc(tam*sizeof(int)));
}

for(i = 0; i < tam; i++)
  for(j = 0; j < tam; j++){
    malha[i][j] = 0;
    malhaTemp[i][j] = 0;
  }


//printf("-----------------------------------\n");

//celulas vivas

for(i = min; i < max; i++)
  for(j = min; j < max; j++)
    malha[i][j] = 1;


/*for(i = 0; i < tam; i++){
  for(j = 0; j < tam; j++){
    printf(" %d ", malha[i][j]);
    }
  printf("\n");
}*/

//celulas vivas

//printf("-----------------------------------\n");

ini = clock();

for(i = 0; i < gera; i++){

  for(j = 0; j < tam; j++){

    for(k = 0; k < tam; k++){

      cont = 0;
      cont += malha[abs((j+1) % tam)][abs((k-1) % tam)];
      cont += malha[abs(j % tam)][abs((k-1) % tam)];
      cont += malha[abs((j-1) % tam)][abs((k-1) % tam)];
      cont += malha[abs((j+1) % tam)][abs(k % tam)];
      cont += malha[abs((j-1) % tam)][abs(k % tam)];
      cont += malha[abs((j+1) % tam)][abs((k+1) % tam)];
      cont += malha[abs(j % tam)][abs((k+1) % tam)];
      cont += malha[abs((j-1) % tam)][abs((k+1) % tam)];
```

```c
      if(cont < 2 && malha[j][k] == 1)
        malhaTemp[j][k] = 0;
      else if (cont == 3 && malha[j][k] == 0)
        malhaTemp[j][k] = 1;
      else if(cont >= 2 && cont <= 3 && malha[j][k] == 1)
        malhaTemp[j][k] = 1;
      else if(cont > 3 && malha[j][k] == 1)
        malhaTemp[j][k] = 0;


    }

  }

  int m,n;
  for(m = 0; m < tam; m++)
    for(n = 0; n < tam; n++)
      malha[m][n] = malhaTemp[m][n];

}

/*for(i = 0; i < tam; i++){
  for(j = 0; j < tam; j++){
    printf(" %d ", malha[i][j]);
    }
  printf("\n");
}*/

fim = clock();

double total = (double)(fim - ini) / CLOCKS_PER_SEC;

FILE *file = fopen("timeC.csv","a+");

if (file != NULL) {
  fprintf(file, "%d;%d;%d;%d;%.06f\n",tam, gera, min, max, total);
}

fclose (file);

//printf("Total - %.04fms\n", total);

return 0;
}
```

Code A.2: Parallel GoL code

```cpp
#include "cuda_runtime.h"
#include "device_launch_parameters.h"
#include <stdio.h>
#include <iostream>
#include <cuda.h>
#include <thrust/version.h>

int threadx, thready, threadz;
int blockx, blocky, blockz;
int warp;
int maxThreadsPerBlock;

using namespace std;

void DisplayHeader()
{
  const int kb = 1024;
  const int mb = kb * kb;

  wcout << "NBody.GPU" << endl << "=========" << endl << endl;

  wcout << "CUDA version:  v" << CUDART_VERSION << endl;
  wcout << "Thrust version: v" << THRUST_MAJOR_VERSION << "." <<
    THRUST_MINOR_VERSION << endl << endl;

  int devCount;
  cudaGetDeviceCount(&devCount);
  wcout << "CUDA Devices: " << endl << endl;

  for(int i = 0; i < devCount; ++i)
  {
    cudaDeviceProp props;
    cudaGetDeviceProperties(&props, i);
    wcout << i << ": " << props.name << ": " << props.major << "." << props.minor
    << endl;
    wcout << " Global memory:  " << props.totalGlobalMem / mb << "mb" << endl;
    wcout << " Shared memory:  " << props.sharedMemPerBlock / kb << "kb" << endl;
    wcout << " Constant memory: " << props.totalConstMem / kb << "kb" << endl;
    wcout << " Block registers: " << props.regsPerBlock << endl << endl;

    wcout << " Warp size:      " << props.warpSize << endl;
    warp = props.warpSize;
    wcout << " Threads per block: " << props.maxThreadsPerBlock << endl;
    maxThreadsPerBlock = props.maxThreadsPerBlock;
    wcout << " Max block dimensions: [ " << props.maxThreadsDim[0] << ", " << props
    .maxThreadsDim[1] << ", " << props.maxThreadsDim[2] << " ]" << endl;
    threadx = props.maxThreadsDim[0];
    thready = props.maxThreadsDim[1];
```

```cpp
      threadz = props.maxThreadsDim[2];
      wcout << " Max grid dimensions: [ " << props.maxGridSize[0] << ", " << props.
          maxGridSize[1] << ", " << props.maxGridSize[2] << " ]" << endl;
      blockx = props.maxGridSize[0];
      blocky = props.maxGridSize[1];
      blockz = props.maxGridSize[2];
      wcout << endl;
  }
}


__global__ void calcViz(const int h_tam, int *d_matrix, int *d_aux){

  int cont;
  int idx = blockIdx.x * blockDim.x + threadIdx.x;
  int idy = blockIdx.y * blockDim.y + threadIdx.y;

  cont = 0;
  cont += d_matrix[((((idx+1)*h_tam)+(idy-1)) % (h_tam*h_tam)];
  cont += d_matrix[(((idx*h_tam)+(idy-1)) % (h_tam*h_tam)];
  cont += d_matrix[((((idx-1)*h_tam)+(idy-1)) % (h_tam*h_tam)];
  cont += d_matrix[((((idx+1)*h_tam)+idy) % (h_tam*h_tam)];
  cont += d_matrix[((((idx-1)*h_tam)+idy) % (h_tam*h_tam)];
  cont += d_matrix[((((idx+1)*h_tam)+(idy+1)) % (h_tam*h_tam)];
  cont += d_matrix[(((idx*h_tam)+(idy+1)) % (h_tam*h_tam)];
  cont += d_matrix[((((idx-1)*h_tam)+(idy+1)) % (h_tam*h_tam)];

  if(cont < 2 && d_matrix[(idx*h_tam)+idy] == 1)
    d_aux[(idx*h_tam)+idy] = 0;
  else if (cont == 3 && d_matrix[(idx*h_tam)+idy] == 0)
    d_aux[(idx*h_tam)+idy] = 1;
  else if (cont >= 2 && cont <= 3 && d_matrix[(idx*h_tam)+idy] == 1)
    d_aux[(idx*h_tam)+idy] = 1;
  else if (cont > 3 && d_matrix[(idx*h_tam)+idy] == 1)
    d_aux[(idx*h_tam)+idy] = 0;

  //__syncthreads();

  d_matrix[(idx*h_tam)+idy] = d_aux[(idx*h_tam)+idy];

  //__syncthreads();

}
int main(int argc, char *argv[]){

  //**********HOST**********//
  int i, j, k, min, max;
  int h_gera;
  int h_ger;
```

```cpp
    int h_tam;
    int **h_matrix;
    //clock_t ini, fim;
    //***********HOST**********//

    //***********DEVICE**********//
    int *d_matrix;
    int *d_aux;
    cudaError_t cudaStatus;
    cudaEvent_t start, stop;
    float elapsedtime;
    //***********DEVICE**********//

    //Exibi info da GPU
    //DisplayHeader();
    threadx = 1024;
    blockx = 65535;
    warp = 32;
    maxThreadsPerBlock = 1024;

    //cout << "Tamanho da matriz: ";
    //cin >> h_tam;
    h_tam = atoi(argv[1]);

    //cout << "Numero de Geracoes: ";
    //cin >> h_gera;
    h_gera = atoi(argv[2]);

    //cout << "Limites das celulas vivas:" << endl;
    //cout << "Min: ";
    //cin >> min;
    min = atoi(argv[3]);
    //cout << "Max: ";
    //cin >> max;
    max = atoi(argv[4]);

    //printf("%d - %d - %d - %d\n\n",h_tam,h_gera,min,max);

    //ini = clock();

    //***********HOST**********//
    int num_elements = h_tam * h_tam;
    int num_bytes = num_elements * sizeof(int);
    int block_sizeX, block_sizeY;
    int grid_sizeX, grid_sizeY;

    /*if(h_tam > (maxThreadsPerBlock/warp))
      block_size = h_tam / ((h_tam / (maxThreadsPerBlock/warp))+(h_tam % (
```

```cpp
      maxThreadsPerBlock/warp)));
else
  block_size = h_tam;

grid_size = h_tam / block_size;*/

block_sizeX = atoi(argv[5]);
block_sizeY = atoi(argv[6]);
grid_sizeX = atoi(argv[7]);
grid_sizeY = atoi(argv[8]);

//***********HOST**********//

//***********DEVICE**********//
dim3 dimBlock(block_sizeX, block_sizeY, 1);
dim3 dimGrid(grid_sizeX, grid_sizeY, 1);
//***********DEVICE**********//

//getchar();

//cout << "Block size: " << block_size << endl;
//cout << "Grid size: " << grid_size << endl;

//getchar();

//aloca matrix
h_matrix = (int**)(malloc(h_tam*sizeof(int*)));
  for( k = 0; k < h_tam; k++)
    h_matrix[k] = (int*)(malloc(h_tam*sizeof(int)));

//inicializa a matrix
for(i = 0; i < h_tam; i++)
  for(j = 0; j < h_tam; j++)
    h_matrix[i][j] = 0;

//inicializa os seres vivos
for(i = min; i < max; i++)
  for(j = min; j < max; j++)
    h_matrix[i][j] = 1;

//aloca vetor
int *h_temp;
h_temp = (int*)(malloc(h_tam*h_tam*sizeof(int)));

//transcreve matrix em vetor
int cont = 0;
for(i = 0; i < h_tam; i++){
  for(j = 0; j < h_tam; j++){
```

```cpp
      h_temp[cont] = h_matrix[i][j];
      //cout << h_temp[cont] << " ";
      cont++;
    }
    //cout << endl;
  }

  //*****************************CUDA*****************************//



  // Choose which GPU to run on, change this on a multi-GPU system.
  cudaStatus = cudaSetDevice(1);
    if(cudaStatus != cudaSuccess){
    cout << "cudaSetDevice failed! Do you have a CUDA-capable GPU installed?" <<
    endl;
    goto Error;
  }

  // Reset GPU.
  cudaStatus = cudaDeviceReset();
    if(cudaStatus != cudaSuccess){
    cout << "cudaDeviceReset failed! Do you have a CUDA-capable GPU installed?" <<
    endl;
    goto Error;
  }

  // Allocate GPU buffers for three vectors (two input, one output)
  cudaStatus = cudaMalloc((void**) &d_matrix, num_bytes);
  if(cudaStatus != cudaSuccess){
    cout << "cudaMalloc failed in d_matrix!" << endl;
    goto Error;
  }

  cudaStatus = cudaMalloc((void**) &d_aux, num_bytes);
  if(cudaStatus != cudaSuccess){
    cout << "cudaMalloc failed in d_aux!" << endl;
    goto Error;
  }

  // Copy input vectors from host memory to GPU buffers.
  cudaStatus = cudaMemcpy( d_matrix, h_temp, num_bytes, cudaMemcpyHostToDevice);
  if(cudaStatus != cudaSuccess){
    cout << "cudaMemcpy failed in d_matrix!" << endl;
    goto Error;
  }

  cudaStatus = cudaMemcpy( d_aux, h_temp, num_bytes, cudaMemcpyHostToDevice);
  if(cudaStatus != cudaSuccess){
```

```cpp
    cout << "cudaMemcpy failed in d_aux!" << endl;
    goto Error;
  }


  h_ger = 0;

  cudaEventCreate(&start);
  cudaEventCreate(&stop);
  cudaEventRecord(start, cudaEventDefault);
  while(h_ger < h_gera){
    // Launch a kernel on the GPU with one thread for each element.
    calcViz <<<dimGrid, dimBlock>>> (h_tam, d_matrix, d_aux);
    cudaDeviceSynchronize();
    h_ger++;

  }
  cudaEventRecord(stop, cudaEventDefault);
  cudaEventSynchronize(start);
  cudaEventSynchronize(stop);
  cudaEventElapsedTime(&elapsedtime, start, stop);
  cudaEventDestroy(start);
  cudaEventDestroy(stop);

  // Check for any errors launching the kernel
  cudaStatus = cudaGetLastError();
  if(cudaStatus != cudaSuccess){
    cout << "calcViz launch failed: " << cudaGetErrorString(cudaStatus) << endl;
    goto Error;
  }

  // cudaDeviceSynchronize waits for the kernel to finish, and returns
  // any errors encountered during the launch.
  cudaStatus = cudaDeviceSynchronize();
  if(cudaStatus != cudaSuccess){
    cout << "cudaDeviceSynchronize returned error code " << cudaStatus << " after
    launching addKernel!" << endl;
    goto Error;
  }

  // Copy output vector from GPU buffer to host memory.
  cudaStatus = cudaMemcpy(h_temp, d_matrix, num_bytes, cudaMemcpyDeviceToHost);
  if(cudaStatus != cudaSuccess){
    cout << "cudaMemcpy failed in d_matrix!" << endl;
    goto Error;
  }

Error:
  //desaloca a matriz no Device
```

```cpp
  cudaFree(d_matrix);
  cudaFree(d_aux);

  cout << endl << "Tempo CUDA: " << elapsedtime << "ms" << endl;

  //************************CUDA************************//

  //cout << endl << "--------------------------------------------------" << endl <<
      endl;

  //atualiza matrix
  /*cont = 0;
  for(i = 0; i < h_tam; i++){
    for(j = 0; j < h_tam; j++){
      h_matrix[i][j] = h_temp[cont];
      cout << h_matrix[i][j] << " ";
      cont++;
    }
    cout << endl;
  }*/

  //cout << "FIM" << endl;
  //getchar();

  FILE *file = fopen("timeCU.csv","a+");

  if (file != NULL) {
    fprintf(file, "%d;%d;%d;%d;%d;%d;%d;%d;%.06f\n",h_tam, h_gera, min, max,
        block_sizeX, block_sizeY, grid_sizeX, grid_sizeY, elapsedtime);
  }

  fclose (file);

  return 0;
}
```

Code A.3: TAC code

```cpp
// nvcc -O3 -arch=compute_20 -code=sm_20,sm_30,sm_35 main.cu -o TAC
#include <iostream>
#include <cstdlib>
#include <cstring>
#include <ctime>
#include <curand_kernel.h>
#include <curand.h>
#include <cstdio>
#include "App.h"
using namespace std;
```

```cpp
#define CHECK_ERROR(call) do {                                    \
  if( cudaSuccess != call) {                                      \
    std::cerr << std::endl << "CUDA ERRO: " <<                    \
      cudaGetErrorString(call) << " in file: " << __FILE__        \
      << " in line: " << __LINE__ << std::endl;                   \
      exit(0);                                                    \
  } } while (0)

struct stConfig{
  float prob;
  int cellX;
  int cellY;
  int vMax;
  bool GPU;
  int typeGPU;
  int steps;
  int nVehicles;
  int blocks;
  int threads;
  bool print;
};

void printGPURoad(int *d_Mesh, int cellX){
  int *h_Mesh = new int [cellX];
  cout << endl;

  CHECK_ERROR(cudaMemcpy(h_Mesh, d_Mesh, cellX * sizeof(int),
      cudaMemcpyDeviceToHost));

  for (int i = 0; i < cellX; i++){
    int v = h_Mesh[i];
    if (v == 0)
      cout << ".";
    else
      cout << "0";


  }
  cout << endl;

  cout.flush();

  delete[] h_Mesh;
  h_Mesh = NULL;


}


__global__ void setup_kernel(const unsigned long long seed, curandState *state){
```

```cpp
  int x    = blockDim.x * blockIdx.x + threadIdx.x;
  curand_init(seed, x, 0, &state[x]);
}


__global__ void updateGPU(int *d_Mesh, int *d_X0){

  const int i = blockIdx.x * blockDim.x + threadIdx.x;
  int v = d_X0[i];
  d_Mesh[v] = i+1;


}




__device__ int NASH_GPU_DIST(int *h_Mesh, const int myX, const int cellX, const int
    vMax){
  int iDist = 0,
    iX = myX,
    iCell = 0;

  do{
    iX++;
    iDist++;
    if (iX == cellX)
      iX = 0;
    iCell = h_Mesh[iX];
  } while ( (iCell == 0) && (iDist < vMax+1));

  int k = (iDist - 1) < 0;

  iDist = (iDist - 1) * (1-k);

  return iDist;
}

__global__ void NASH_GPU (int *d_V1,
              int *d_V0,
              int *d_Mesh,
              int *d_X0,
              curandState *state,
              const int cellX,
              const int nVehicles,
              const int vMax,
              const float prob){

  int k = 0,
    d = 0;
```

```c
    float r = 0.0f;
    const int i = blockIdx.x * blockDim.x + threadIdx.x;

      k = (d_V0[i] + 1) > vMax;
      d_V1[i] = ((d_V0[i] + 1) * (1-k)) + (vMax * k);


      d = NASH_GPU_DIST(d_Mesh, d_X0[i] , cellX, vMax);


      k = d_V1[i] > d;


      d_V1[i] = (d * k) + (d_V1[i] * (1-k));



      r = curand_uniform(&state[i]);


      k = (r < prob) & (d_V1[i] > 0);



      d_V1[i] = ((d_V1[i] - 1) * k) + (d_V1[i] * (1-k));;

}


__global__ void NASH_UPDATE_GPU( int *d_X1,
                    int *d_X0,
                    int *d_V1,
                    const int nVehicles,
                    const int cellX){
  int k = 0;
  const int i = blockIdx.x * blockDim.x + threadIdx.x;

  d_X1[i] = d_X0[i] + d_V1[i];
  k = (d_X1[i] >= cellX);
  d_X1[i] = ((d_X1[i] - cellX) * k) + (d_X1[i] * (1-k));




}


void GPU(stConfig config){
    int   *h_X0 = NULL,
        *d_Mesh = NULL,
        *d_X0 = NULL,
        *d_X1 = NULL,
        *d_V0 = NULL,
        *d_V1 = NULL;
```

```cpp
curandState    *d_States = NULL;
Stopwatch sw;
FREQUENCY(sw);


cout << "Working on GPU: " << config.typeGPU << endl;
CHECK_ERROR(cudaSetDevice(config.typeGPU));
CHECK_ERROR(cudaDeviceReset());


h_X0 = new int [config.nVehicles];

CHECK_ERROR(cudaMalloc((void**) &d_Mesh, config.cellX * sizeof(int)));
CHECK_ERROR(cudaMalloc((void**) &d_X0, config.nVehicles * sizeof(int)));
CHECK_ERROR(cudaMalloc((void**) &d_X1, config.nVehicles * sizeof(int)));
CHECK_ERROR(cudaMalloc((void**) &d_V0, config.nVehicles * sizeof(int)));
CHECK_ERROR(cudaMalloc((void**) &d_V1, config.nVehicles * sizeof(int)));
CHECK_ERROR(cudaMalloc((void**) &d_States, config.nVehicles * sizeof(
    curandState)));


//Initial condition
bzero(h_X0, config.nVehicles * sizeof(int));

CHECK_ERROR(cudaMemset(d_Mesh, 0, config.cellX * sizeof(int)));
CHECK_ERROR(cudaMemset(d_X1, 0, config.nVehicles * sizeof(int)));
CHECK_ERROR(cudaMemset(d_V0, 0, config.nVehicles * sizeof(int)));
CHECK_ERROR(cudaMemset(d_V1, 0, config.nVehicles * sizeof(int)));

for (int i = 0; i < config.nVehicles; i++)
  h_X0[i] = i;

CHECK_ERROR(cudaMemcpy(d_X0, h_X0, config.nVehicles * sizeof(int),
  cudaMemcpyHostToDevice));
setup_kernel<<< config.blocks, config.threads >>>(time (NULL), d_States);
//printGPURoad(d_Mesh, config.cellX);
cout << endl << endl;

START_STOPWATCH(sw);
for (int i = 0; i < config.steps; i++){
  CHECK_ERROR(cudaMemset(d_Mesh, 0, config.cellX * sizeof(int)));
  updateGPU<<<config.blocks, config.threads>>>    (d_Mesh, d_X0);
  if (config.print)
    printGPURoad(d_Mesh, config.cellX);
  NASH_GPU<<<config.blocks, config.threads>>>    (d_V1, d_V0, d_Mesh, d_X0,
      d_States, config.cellX, config.nVehicles, config.vMax, config.prob);
  NASH_UPDATE_GPU<<<config.blocks, config.threads>>> (d_X1, d_X0, d_V1, config.
      nVehicles, config.cellX);
```

```cpp
        int *ptr = NULL;
        ptr = d_X0;
        d_X0 = d_X1;
        d_X1 = ptr;

        ptr = d_V0;
        d_V0 = d_V1;
        d_V1 = ptr;

    }

    CHECK_ERROR(cudaDeviceSynchronize());
    STOP_STOPWATCH(sw);
    cout << "Elapsedtime: " << sw.mElapsedTime << " ms" << endl;
    string name = "ResultsGTX570.csv";
    FILE *file = fopen(name.c_str(),"a+");
    fprintf(file, "%f %d %d %d %d %d %d %f\n", config.prob, config.nVehicles,
        config.cellX, config.GPU, config.blocks, config.threads, config.steps, sw.
        mElapsedTime);
    fclose (file);

    CHECK_ERROR(cudaFree(d_Mesh));
    CHECK_ERROR(cudaFree(d_X0));
    CHECK_ERROR(cudaFree(d_X1));
    CHECK_ERROR(cudaFree(d_V0));
    CHECK_ERROR(cudaFree(d_V1));
    CHECK_ERROR(cudaFree(d_States));

}

/*
 * CPU version
 */
void printConfig(stConfig config);
void printCPURoad(int *h_Mesh, int *h_X0, int *h_V0, int cellX, int nVehicles);
int NASH_CPU_DIST(int *h_Mesh, int myX, int cellX, int vMax);
void NASH_UPDATE_CPU( int *h_X1, int *h_X0, int *h_V1, int nVehicles, int cellX);
void NASH_CPU(int *h_V1, int *h_V0, int *h_Mesh, int *h_X0, int cellX, int
    nVehicles, int vMax, float prob);
void updateCPU(int *h_Mesh, int *h_X0, int cellX, int nVehicles);
void CPU(stConfig config);

int main (int argc, char **argv){
  stConfig config;

  config.prob = atof(argv[1]); //0.25f;
```

```cpp
  config.nVehicles = atoi(argv[2]); //100000
  config.cellX = atoi(argv[3]); //config.nVehicles * 4;
  config.cellY = atoi(argv[4]); //1;
  config.vMax = atoi(argv[5]);// 5;
  config.GPU = atoi(argv[6]); //false;
  config.typeGPU = atoi(argv[7]); //0;
  config.blocks = atoi(argv[8]); //1;
  config.threads = atoi(argv[9]); //config.nVehicles;
  config.steps = atoi(argv[10]); //config.nVehicles * 10;
  config.print = atoi(argv[11]); //false;

  printConfig(config);


  if (config.GPU)
    GPU(config);
  else
    CPU(config);

  return EXIT_SUCCESS;
}


void printConfig(stConfig config){
  cout << "NASCH model simulation:" << endl << endl;
  cout << "\t    prob:" << config.prob << endl;
  cout << "\t    cellX:" << config.cellX << endl;
  cout << "\t    cellY:" << config.cellY << endl;
  cout << "\t    vMax:" << config.vMax << endl;
  cout << "\t     GPU:" << config.GPU << endl;

  cout << "\t    steps:" << config.steps << endl;
  cout << "\t nVehicles:" << config.nVehicles << endl;
  if (config.GPU){
    cout << "\t\t   typeGPU:" << config.typeGPU << endl;
    cout << "\t\t   blocks:" << config.blocks << endl;
    cout << "\t\t   threads:" << config.threads << endl;

  }
  cout << endl << endl << endl;

}

void printCPURoad(int *h_Mesh, int *h_XO, int *h_VO, int cellX, int nVehicles){
  cout << endl;
  for (int i = 0; i < cellX; i++){
    int v = h_Mesh[i];
    if (v == 0)
```

```cpp
        cout << ".";
      else
        cout << "0";


  }
  cout << endl;

  cout.flush();

}

int NASH_CPU_DIST(int *h_Mesh, int myX, int cellX, int vMax){
  int iDist = 0,
    iX = myX,
    iCell = 0;

  do{
    iX++;
    iDist++;
    if (iX == cellX)
      iX = 0;
    iCell = h_Mesh[iX];
  } while ( (iCell == 0) && (iDist < vMax+1));

  int k = (iDist - 1) < 0;

  iDist = (iDist - 1) * (1-k);

  return iDist;
}

void NASH_UPDATE_CPU( int *h_X1, int *h_X0, int *h_V1, int nVehicles, int cellX){
  int k = 0;
  for (int i = 0; i < nVehicles; i++){
    h_X1[i] = h_X0[i] + h_V1[i];
    k = (h_X1[i] >= cellX);
    h_X1[i] = ((h_X1[i] - cellX) * k) + (h_X1[i] * (1-k));



  }
}

void NASH_CPU(int *h_V1, int *h_V0, int *h_Mesh, int *h_X0, int cellX, int
    nVehicles, int vMax, float prob){
  int k = 0,
    d = 0;
```

```cpp
  float r = 0.0f;
  for (int i = 0; i < nVehicles; i++){

    k = (h_V0[i] + 1) > vMax;
    h_V1[i] = ((h_V0[i] + 1) * (1-k)) + (vMax * k);
    d = NASH_CPU_DIST(h_Mesh, h_X0[i] , cellX, vMax);
    k = h_V1[i] > d;

    h_V1[i] = (d * k) + (h_V1[i] * (1-k));


    r = static_cast <float> (rand() % 65535 + 1) / 65535.0f;
    k = (r < prob) & (h_V1[i] > 0);


    h_V1[i] = ((h_V1[i] - 1) * k) + (h_V1[i] * (1-k));;

  }

}

void updateCPU(int *h_Mesh, int *h_X0, int cellX, int nVehicles){
  bzero(h_Mesh, cellX * sizeof(int));
  for (int i = 0; i < nVehicles; i++){
      int v = h_X0[i];

      h_Mesh[v] = i+1;
  }

}

void CPU(stConfig config){
  int *h_Mesh = NULL,
    *h_V0 = NULL,
    *h_X0 = NULL,
    *h_V1 = NULL,
    *h_X1 = NULL;

  Stopwatch sw;
  FREQUENCY(sw);

  h_Mesh = new int [config.cellX];
  h_V0 = new int [config.nVehicles];
  h_V1 = new int [config.nVehicles];
  h_X0 = new int [config.nVehicles];
  h_X1 = new int [config.nVehicles];
```

```cpp
  srand (time(NULL));

  //Initial condition
  bzero(h_Mesh, config.cellX * sizeof(int));
  bzero(h_V0, config.nVehicles * sizeof(int));
  bzero(h_V1, config.nVehicles * sizeof(int));
  bzero(h_X0, config.nVehicles * sizeof(int));
  bzero(h_X1, config.nVehicles * sizeof(int));

  for (int i = 0; i < config.nVehicles; i++)
    h_X0[i] = i;

  //printCPURoad(h_Mesh, h_X0, h_V0, config.cellX, config.nVehicles);
  cout << endl << endl;


  START_STOPWATCH(sw);
  for (int i = 0; i < config.steps; i++){


    updateCPU(h_Mesh, h_X0, config.cellX, config.nVehicles);

    if (config.print) printCPURoad(h_Mesh, h_X0, h_V0, config.cellX, config.
        nVehicles);

    NASH_CPU(h_V1, h_V0, h_Mesh, h_X0, config.cellX, config.nVehicles, config.vMax,
        config.prob);
    NASH_UPDATE_CPU(h_X1, h_X0, h_V1, config.nVehicles, config.cellX);

    int *ptr = NULL;
    ptr = h_X0;
    h_X0 = h_X1;
    h_X1 = ptr;

    ptr = h_V0;
    h_V0 = h_V1;
    h_V1 = ptr;


  }
  STOP_STOPWATCH(sw);
  cout << "Elapsedtime: " << sw.mElapsedTime << " ms" << endl;

  string name = "ResultsGTX570.csv";
  FILE *file = fopen(name.c_str(),"a+");
  fprintf(file, "%f %d %d %d %d %d %d %f\n", config.prob, config.nVehicles, config.
      cellX, config.GPU, config.blocks, config.threads, config.steps, sw.
      mElapsedTime);
```

```cpp
    fclose (file);

    delete [] h_Mesh;
    delete [] h_X0;
    delete [] h_V0;
    delete [] h_X1;
    delete [] h_V1;

}
```

Buy your books fast and straightforward online - at one of world's fastest growing online book stores! Environmentally sound due to Print-on-Demand technologies.

Buy your books online at
www.morebooks.shop

Kaufen Sie Ihre Bücher schnell und unkompliziert online – auf einer der am schnellsten wachsenden Buchhandelsplattformen weltweit! Dank Print-On-Demand umwelt- und ressourcenschonend produziert.

Bücher schneller online kaufen
www.morebooks.shop

info@omniscriptum.com
www.omniscriptum.com

Printed by Books on Demand GmbH, Norderstedt / Germany